# LEARN TO

# HEAR

# FROM LISTENING

# by THE RUNNER

LEARN TO HEAR FROM LISTENING
THE RUNNER

First Printing 2005

ISBN: 9780986237379

Printed in the United States of America

# Learn To Hear From Listening

# Table of Contents

**Motivational Reading**

**Learn to Hear From Listening**

**Acknowledgements**

All thanks to God, my parents, and my daughters.  To Dr. Richard Taylor, my English professor who told me I had the gift to become a writer.  Paul Robinson, who gave me a writing pad and a pencil.  To the guys with their input from Northpoint Training Center upon my arrival.  To my sister LaTonya and Juliann K. for typing this book to help our youth across the world.  Oh, also I must thank my horse family:  grandfather, Getty's, Frankie Brother's, Bobby, Eukie, James, Nick Zito, Shug McGauhey, Seth Hancock, Elliott Walden, Doc Danner, Ronnie Eubanks aka E.B., Shane Sellers, Todd Pletcher, Coach Wayne Lukas, Bertrand, Doctor Jackie Shellow, Ronnie and Dee Holassie and Rick and JoAnn Pitino for letting me into their world!  Thanks for letting me learn to hear from listening and seeing to believe.

# Preface

First of all, this book is not based on religion, but it is based on truth and the truth is important to you and your friends or family members. Even for your enemies it is important to learn to hear[1] from listening. You must learn to listen[2] because if you do not, your life can become very miserable and therefore, it is my hopes that this message reaches you as it has myself.

*Incline your ear and hear the words of the wise and apply your heart to God's knowledge; for it is a pleasant thing if you keep them with you; let them all be fixed upon your lips.*

Learn to Hear from Listening is based on a true story. However, the characters are fictional.

***Author: The Runner***

## Chapter 1 – Prison Talk
## Thinking Street Game was My Success

I'm sitting here at Northpoint Training Center on March 23, 2003 and would like to thank God for giving me the courage to write this short motivational book because here you must stay motivated to survive in the land of the maniacs. So, I'll start by asking, "Why don't we listen and hear what our parents tell and try to teach us?"

In my family I was taught to respect my parents and to respect God. Well, I did both of those things until I was fourteen years old and then it was my way or at least that's what I thought. I rebelled against my parents for getting a divorce and then against God for allowing it to happen. My attitude became terrible towards everybody and I was just the opposite of what I was taught to be. I thought my rebellion would hurt others, but I was really only hurting myself. I went from being an A and B student academically to failing purposely.

Growing up we lived next door to the YMCA, so at the ages of eleven and twelve I became very athletic. I played basketball, football, baseball, softball, boxing and I even took karate. In team sports we united as one to win championships however, it was something about the age of fourteen that had me believing I didn't have to listen ot hear and hear what my parents, teachers, or coaches were trying to teach me.

I stopped attending church and stopped getting down on my knees every night; praying before I went to bed. Twenty-six years later – this is where I'm at. God brought me back into His world to let you all know that this is not the place for you to come. If you are willing to take my advice you will not come here because prison is full of sick and lazy people. It is full of murderers, rapists, child molesters, drug dealers, user's and last, but not least, thieves. Sadly, some of these guys do not want to live in society because they've been incarcerated so long they are now instutionalized.

Life is too short to not listen and hear the truth. It may not be what you want to hear at the time, but it will save you from coming to prison or getting killed. To me we were born to die so why get killed when you have the opportunity to live and die in peace? In my opinion, dying in prison would be like committing suicide because it was ultimately my choices and/or actions that landed me here.

Thanks be to God that He has given me another chance. A chance that some of these guys don't and won't get because they are here until their hearts stop beating; meaning until death.

Youngsters, you all have a chance to put the prison system in a low capacity and that is by doing the right thing. Learn to hear from listening to what is right or else you will keep the prison system over populated. Once you enter into the prison world you can't leave until they say you can. Like I stated earlier, some inmates will never get to enjoy freedom again. So, if you do not want to spend your precious days on this earth with some punk in a bunk or have guards tell you when to eat, shower, and when to sleep you must start by making a conscious effort to change your wrong ways to the right way. I believe this is accomplished by loving thy neighbor as well as thy enemy, and promoting peace on this wonderful earth as I am now trying to do.

My short stay in prison, which is a three-year sentence, feels like an eternity. I keep praying that I make it to the day that I walk out of here in one piece. Free from bondage. I've seen a couple of fights and it makes me sick; along with hearing a rapist sodomizing his next victim. Remember what I said, "This is the land of the maniacs."

Allow me to tell you about about Derby Eve, May of 2000. I met a female (this happened before my incarceration) named Holly at a sports bar in Louisville, Kentucky, and we befriended one another. She took me to her apartment where she had a picture of her boyfriend, whom she said was in prison and wanted her to come visit him on Derby day. However, me being selfish, I made a statement to her that if I was in prison I wouldn't want any visitors. Well, this goes back to when my mother would say, "Son do not talk about other people because what goes around comes back around twice as hard."

I wrote Holly and told her that I was *still* in prison. My mother made a believer out of me. If only I had learned to hear and listen to what she had said. May her soul rest in peace.

It is my belief that if the gangs make redemption by hearing and listening to Stanley Williams, surely we can make an effort to promote world peace to stop terrorism and gorillalism by countries, including the U.S.A., by facing the reality that we are all God's (Allah's) children. Therefore, I've begun a new journey which does not consist of violence, drugs, guns, or negative behavior. It will consist of peace and positive influence to our youth of today (who are our future).

Young people, we need for you all to take a stand and work with each other to promote world peace on this earth. No matter what color, religion, financial background, or gender you are. We're all family and it has been that way since the beginning of life. Our ancestors came up with a negative idea to divide and conquer each other with hate and greed for material gain.

When I say divide, I mean by race, religion, education, materially, and financially. Bottom line is, we should look at everyone equally and not passing judgment on anyone. This, to me, can be done by following the example set by the annual Hajj in Mecca where the people wear simple clothes, which strip away distinctions of class and culture, so that all stand equal before God.

We want you, our youth, to grow up and be husbands, wives, doctors, and lawyers or whatever you set your mind to being as long as it's positive. Prison does not make you a man and it is not gladiator school. Prison is designed to lead us astray so that once we get here we become lazy and institutionalized. This means that we're lost forever and the system should not be used in this manner, yet for purposes of rehabilitation.

## Thinking Street Game was My Success

When you grow up playing sports people have a tendency to flock to you or want you to hang out with them. At the age of thirteen I had become pretty good at sports and it seems that as a result of that the street life was introduced to me early. I had older guys offering me knowledge e.g. how to play craps, simply because I had a mean jump shot.

Craps is a game where two dice are numbered one through six with a total of twelve between the two. If you roll seven or eleven on your first roll, you win, but if you roll two, three, or twelve on your first roll, you lose. If you roll any other number, for instance six, on your first roll then that is called your point.

You have to continue rolling the dice until six comes up, but if seven comes before six you lose. Well, I became pretty lucky in the game until I was taught a lesson by an older player named Scoot. I beat him out of all his money and then he went and borrowed some more money, came back and wanted a rematch. My young greed got the best of me. He took me up to his apartment and slipped a crooked dice in the game and won all of his money back. Plus my money!

He later told me he used the crooked dice to teach me a lesson about trash talking. Crooked dice are dice made with certain numbers on them to either miss or hit. Well, after Scoot taught me my first lesson, I started using this method on others in the crap games.  However, it was short lived due to an incident I witnessed where a guy made a mistake while trying to slip the crooked dice into a game which resulted in his teeth being kicked out of his mouth.

Needless to say, my crap game success ended as I thought of how that could have been me.  The experience took me back to the basic teachings I was taught by my parents.  My father said, "Son, do not gamble unless it's a fair game."  I didn't hear him.

Then came the red card known as *Three Card Monte*.  This game is played with three cards; two of the same black suit, such as: two black kings of spades and one king of heart.  The object of the game is to find the red card and not the black one.  An older guy, Junie, taught Ray and myself this game.  Junie was an ex-basketball star at DuValle Junior High School in Louisville, Kentucky, who saw our basketball potential.

Junie gave us an audience, not only to display our basketball skills, but also as an opportunity to make some extra money with the red card.  In the game you're not cheating, but people sure do think you are because the hands are quicker than the eye.  This game also lets you know who is greedier for money because they will bet almost anything of value thinking they're going to win.  Well, my mother used to say, "Son, be careful because everyone is not a good loser," but I didn't listen to hear what she was saying.

I threw the cards one time too many and won against a man who didn't lose well.  He pulled a shotgun out on me and demanded his money back. I was literally scared straight to the point that I stopped playing *Three Card Monte* as well.

By now I've learned that my little head also gets hard and I was able to use it on females as well as my hands and tongue. I became a womanizer because I took care of their bodies like I was serving up an appetizer, entrée, and dessert. This allowed me to receive money, automobiles, clothes, drugs, and trips out of town.

The few Queens that I was blessed to have in my life I took their kindness for a weakness because some of them had boyfriends and/or husbands and was taking money and drugs from them to give to me. I also had a few of the Queens that would steal from stores to clothe me without my twisting their arms to do so. There were a couple of women who would sell weed and cocaine as a result of me giving them sexual pleasure and satisfaction which got them sprung.

My point is that I used to talk about people who stole and did drugs and then I became a weed, cocaine user, and also a thief. While engaging in the use of drugs, at first for recreational purposes, I got my girlfriend's friend pregnant. I was under the influence and wasn't able to reason logically and made some terrible mistakes as a result of drug use. Bottom line goes back to the basic teaching. Do not pass judgment on another person because we are not God! I learned to hear from listening.

As a thief my game progressed and was introduced to picking pockets. This trade became pretty prosperous to me until one

Derby Eve I saw a picketer go into an undercover police detective's pocket at a concert, and then ran out of the concert venue. I gave up the pick pocketing when I realized that the street game was not my claim to fame!

I'm going to make this short and simple. We all have a common bond and that is the blood that flows through our veins. Therefore, in my opinion, that makes us family and we're all here by the grace of God. So, why not play together, as kids would do in one big playpen, and spread peace throughout the earth instead of war.

Let's make peace and try to get along with one another. We need to spread love around the world so that our kids and their kids and their kids' kids will be able to live as one. Let's make the difference and change our way of living and promote peace on earth until we pass away from this life.

The Runner

## Chapter II – Prison Talk From David

Hi, my name is David, and I'm here in 2003 at the Northpoint Training Center. I was born October 11, 1973 in New York City with both of my parents in the household. My mother was a school teacher and my father was a school teacher and a counselor. My family believes in God and goes to church almost every Sunday. While I was growing up in the city I got exposed to a lot of scenery e.g. witnessing crime, pimps, hustlers, drug pushers and users.

When this adventure began for me I was eleven years old. After school I would go down to my Uncle Kevin's bar and ask him if I could sweep up the place while I watched guys shoot pool on the side. One day I went to Uncle Kevin's place and went into the bathroom. When I entered a voice coming from the toilet stall said to me, "Yo, come over here." I went to see who it was and it was Leonard, the best pool shooter I had seen at my age.

He asked me if I wanted to make twenty dollars. Leonard took a piece of rubber, wrapped it tight around his arm until a vein popped out. He wanted me to stick the needle he had in his hand into the vein and told me not to tell anyone. So, I did *and* I didn't tell anyone. From that day forward, when Mr. Leonard saw me at Uncle Kevin's or on the street he'd give me a bet; some money. It would be around ten or twenty dollars.

Mr. Leonard was a very sharp dresser, with a new Cadillac, women and always had a wad of money in his pocket. This materialistic type of stuff excited me. So, from that day on I wanted to be like Mr. Leonard which was odd because my parents were like the Cleavers; always wanting to eat together and go to the movies as a family, but for me this became boring after seeing the excitement at Uncle Kevin's place.

Time went on. I was passing in school and had turned several years older. I'm about fourteen now and already six feet tall, but I wasn't into sports. I was into the hustle game. I learned from my Uncle Kevin and Mr. Leonard how to become a pretty good pool player. So, I started hustling and shooting pool around the city and earning extra cash. I began buying hip-hop fashionwear with my allowance and hustle money instead of looking like a preppy nerd.

One evening I came home to have my parents meet me at the entrance of my house. They asked me if everything was alright with me. I responded, "Sure. Why?" They said, "We were just wondering where this three hundred dollars came from that was underneath your mattress?"

The envelope the money was in fell on the floor when my mom changed my linen. I told them I had been saving my extra money from Uncle Kevin's. They asked, "He's paying you that much money?" I responded, "I've been saving for a long time." That day, November 19, 1987, marked the first day that I lied to my parents. Uncle Kevin, my mom's brother, covered for me and said he had given me extra money for Christmas.

Now, it's my sixteenth birthday party on October 11, 1989, and I'm selling heroine for Mr. Leonard, making more money than I'd ever made before. Because it was my sixteenth birthday I could now get my driver's license and purchase a car. I had been praying for the day that I could purchase an automobile and floss for the ladies.

Well, I went and took my driver's test and passed it. Then I asked my parents to help me purchase a car because they had no clue of me selling heroine or else they would have personally turned me into the police! My mom and dad said they would help with the purchase, but I would have to finish high school first. However, I could not wait two more years, so I took the money I had and went to Mr. Leonard and asked him to take me. Mr. Leonard said okay, that we could do it Saturday.

Well, Saturday came and we went to a friend of Mr. Leonard's, who owned a used car lot, and purchased me a nice 1985 Maxima. It was black with beige interior, automatic, five-star rims, low mileage and in mint condition. My attitude was, "I'm going to have so much trim coming my way that I'm going to need a bouncer to get rid of the girls I didn't choose to be with." Plus, all the player hating dudes were jealous of me anyway for being a money-making youngster.

I drove my new car home to find my parents asking why did I go out and purchase a car without their permission. This caused division between me and my parents and I moved out. I dropped out of school and found me a nice, low priced apartment. While in my apartment building I met a very nice female who happened to be four years older than me. Her name was Savannah. She seemed so sweet and innocent so I asked her if I could take her out to eat and to the movies. She accepted my invitation.

I took her to Bennigan's restaurant, then we went to see Batman. While the evening went on we were getting to know each other. She told me that she's attending Julliard School of Dance and that her dream was to dance in Broadway musicals. Savannah said she came from a broken, single parent home, but she received a scholarship to the school. Savannah told me her mom encouraged her by saying, "if you have a dream to be a dancer then fulfill your dreams by going for it," and that is why she came to New York from Washington, D.C.

Our evening went on to start the beginning of our friendship. Oh, by the way, she asked me what I did for a living at my age. I had become so good at lying, that I told her I was twenty-one and worked for a Horse Transportation Company, transporting horses as an attendant up and down the east coast.

About a month later, Savannah saw me come into the building and asked me if I wanted to come over to her place for dinner and a movie. So, I took her up on her offer. We had dinner and she told me to make myself at home. To my surprise she pulled out a dish with a lid on it. She lifted the lid and "Whoa," I said. It was heroine. Savannah snorted some of the heroine, then she asked me to try some, however from my dealings with heroine, I never had the urge to try it. But on this night she was looking so good, in her sexy lingerie, she could have asked me to do just about anything.

I tried the heroine. I put a straw up to my nose and I began to snort. Well, I snorted more than I should have because I became sick and started vomiting up all the food I had eaten that day. All I could remember was hearing Savannah say, "its okay. You just snorted too much, baby. You'll be okay."

I woke the next morning bare naked in her bed. We began to have passionate sex and with my penis keeping a hard on, it seemed to last longer than usual.

Well, from that day on, Savannah and I became a couple and I looked forward to snorting heroine so I could have good sex with her. I even told her the truth about my job and started going in my own packs. While dating Savannah I learned that she supported her habit by being an exotic dancer on the weekends at a strip club, which was for high rollers; high money-making rollers.

My tolerance became high; therefore I needed to snort more heroine. My money started getting short toward re-upping and Mr.

Leonard was asking me what was going on with me because he mentioned my attitude and money had changed. He asked me was I using and if I was that I should quit immediately. My response was, "Mr. Leonard, you use." He said it was something he wanted to do in his life. It just so happened that he was forced into taking heroine when he wanted to become a gang-banger - that was their initiation back when he was coming up in the seventies.

In my case, I was coaxed by a female to put heroine in my system. She identified my weakness. She knew I was wanting sex from her and knew seeing her in that sexy lingerie would make me do anything to get her out of it.

On the night she had me over for dinner and a movie that was my downfall toward self-destruction. At the time it occurred I didn't even see it coming. I thought I was being a cool cat. Now, it is the year 1992 and I am nineteen years of age and a stone-cold heroine junkie. I am stealing just about anything worth some money to support my heroin habit, also I'm now an intravenous user; which is twice as addictive as snorting heroine.

My addiction caused me to become very good at shoplifting clothes from major department stores. I tried to steal any name brand for my connect (supplier) because they would give me half price of the garment cost. I would only steal items such as Polo, Tommy Hilfiger, Coach, Gucci, Sean Jean, Roca Wear, Ecko, and computers. But as they say, every good dog has its day.

# The Runner

The store finally got me. I was caught with six leather Polo jackets while trying to leave the store. I was arrested and put in jail for about three days and I got real sick because I didn't have any heroine, I couldn't eat any food and I was curled up in a ball, in my bunk, shivering and shaking. When I went to court, because it was my first offense, I received three years' probation and was told to stay out of the store I was caught shoplifting in or else my probation would be revoked.

Now, I have to take my show on the road unless I wanted to go up state for three years. When I got released from jail, I could not wait to get a fix. So, I went to the dope man and asked him for some credit. Oh, by the way, Mr. Leonard had cut off dealings with me a few years before, when I wouldn't listen to him. I wish I had learned to hear from listening to him.

Well, the dope man did give me some credit because he knew I would go out later when I got myself together, plus, I always kept him in the best outfits.

This process of going back and forth to jail continued for about ten years, until I landed myself in the county one too many times. I was sentenced here at Northpoint Training Center serving a six year sentence, plus had to enrol in a drug program that was required of my plea because if I didn't, I was looking at a persistent felony offender charge, which carried an extra five to ten years on my sentence.

Believe it or not, I feel like the system, here in Kentucky, saved my life.

I was running from state to state and city to city on my stealing sprees to support my heroin addiction. This could have cost me my life with the different situations I put myself in just because I was trying to impress a good-looking older female for sex. Now, that I'm here at Northpoint and my mind and body have healed, I can appreciate being here. I want to do positive things with my new life now. I've even gotten my GED.

I have also enrolled in carpentry school to obtain a trade so that I can be productive in society when, and if, I walk out these doors to freedom. You don't want to listen or hear what people have to say when your way is working, but when you have to play by somebody else's rules, and if your intentions are to get out of their system, you must play by their rules and learn to hear and listen. You will appreciate it in the long run.

My message to the youth of today is if you have someone who is giving you positive advice, take it as a compliment because they are trying to keep you all from wasting your lives. Get involved in school, church, academics, sports and working to achieve positive goals in life.

Understand that life is too short for us to throw it away on negative issues such as crime, drugs to sell, drugs to use and hanging out with people who do not want to progress positively in life. If you all would like to be able to vote, raise kids, have a nice home or homes, you all must understand that nothing worth something is going to be easy. Life is a continuous struggle in my opinion. My life is not based on religion but when you bow down and do God's will, each and every day you live your life will be much better because God knows it is a continuous struggle serving Him.

Young people, all I'm asking is that you all understand that you have a choice to do right or wrong. You can get help from all types of resources, especially if you are not getting positive advice from home, school, work, relatives or friends. If I had it to do all over again, I would have listened to my parents sooner instead of later. We must realize that our parents love us and will sometimes tell us things that we do not want to hear, however, the majority of the time they are looking out for our best interest.

We, as young teenagers, think that they are trying to take over our lives, but that is so far from the truth. They are simply trying to steer us in the right direction, showing us the importance in the decisions that we make and the paths that we choose to pursue.

You can believe me when I say that this time, when and if I am able to walk out the doors of this place, I am going to make my life simple and that is to obey the laws of the land and apologize to my parents face to face. I plan on getting me a job in my trade, which I received here at Northpoint Training Center.

Young people, it is not about being tough or trying to impress females or even your peers. It is about doing what is right by our conscious. I would like to thank Mr. Runner for letting me share some of my life with you all. Hopefully, my information will help you become a better person. I was told that Watana is now drug free and teaches dance to under privileged kids. As for Mr. Earl, he has been to prison and lives in a homeless shelter and attends Narcotics and Alcoholic Anonymous meetings.

## Chapter III – Prison Talk From Craig

Hello, my name is Craig and I'm here at Northpoint Training Center. The date is March 2003. I was born on August 3, 1969, in Washington, D.C., but I caught time in Louisville, Kentucky for trafficking cocaine. I was a first time offender and received twenty years because some of the cocaine I possessed was "ready rock," which carries more time.

I was raised in a single parent home. My mother and I lived in a housing project in Washington, D.C. where I was exposed to drugs, guns, pimps, hoes and death. By the time I was ten, the year was 1979, I knew just about all the hookers in the neighborhood mainly because my mother was one. She would have the girls over to our apartment partying and buying clothes from one of our neighbors, Paul, who was a booster.

He was the neighborhood thief who could get first class clothes and then sell them to the girls for the low. What little money their pimps would leave them with or did not know about, the ladies would use to purchase clothing items that would make them look good. Even though all of mama's girlfriends were fine, the clothes made them look even finer.

What impressed me most about them was the way they treated their pimps. I mean, the pimps had these girls giving them money without thinking twice. That was so incredible to me at the age of ten and especially since the money was so hard to come by in our neighborhood.

Most of the women in my hood were on welfare and would get a check every first of the month, unless they had a baby daddy with a job that was willing to help with support. The other employment options were to either pimp hoes, sell drugs, rob or steal for a living. Back then I found that the sad part of it all was this was the only way to survive at that stage in my life. I wanted to be just like those guys because they were my heroes.

In 1983 I was celebrating my fourteenth birthday. My mother's pimp, Sonny Boy, stood six foot tall, brown complexion, and had that good hair. He was very suave. He took a liking to me and was the closest thing I had to a father figure in my life. On that day Sonny Boy got me the best gift I thought a fourteen-year-old boy could ever get. He had one of his prostitutes break my virginity.

I mean it was, at the time, a new beginning for me because she taught me the art of sex or making love to the female body. I mastered the trade, and then started taking advantage of females from my age on up into their early twenties. The next thing I knew they were taking care of me, selling their bodies, giving me money, and buying me clothes. I was the sharpest dresser in my school.

I was wearing Bally Alligator shoes, Polo, Izod, silk undershirts and pants. My wardrobe was so solid that I gave my old clothes to some of my boys in the hood. All this money and material stuff was coming to me just for providing good sex to females and I thought that was the life planned for me thanks to Mr. Pimp - Sonny Boy.

When I turned sixteen I seen Sonny Boy beat one of the prostitutes for coming up short with his money and my thoughts about him changed. My mother always told me if I had to beat a woman, then I didn't need her. Besides, I never saw Mr. Sonny Boy hit my mother because she was good at what she did, plus it was good money with her being a single parent.

The reason I decided not to be a pimp was because I confronted Mr. Sonny Boy about whooping this prostitute named, Tammy, and he told me that it came with the territory. If you didn't administer a light beating to them when they cheated you, your pimp days would be short lived. Plus, I found out he was giving the girls dope, even my mother, who kept her addiction from me until I started looking for signs and noticing how she would fall off to sleep for minutes and then wake right up like she was in a trance. She would then go out and handle her business.

She always told me not to get involved with drugs, as a user or seller, but I felt betrayed because she lied to me and the drugs didn't seem to harm her. So, I started selling heroin to make more money. I had never imagined so many people used heroin. My intentions were to sell enough heroin to get me and my mother out of the projects and into a nice neighborhood and a house that would belong to us and not to the housing projects or no pimp.

I came to hate Mr. Pimp because of what he stood for until my mother confronted me and said Mr. Pimp did not make her use drugs.  She told me she was doing them before she met him and that my father was the one who put the needle in her arm.  So, then my rage turned toward him.

My mother said that Mr. Pimp helped her slow down and clean up because if it wasn't for him she didn't know what would have come of her life.  I changed my attitude about Mr. Pimp, but I decided I wasn't going to be one because I was not built like that.  My game was the dope game; the users were already users and I didn't have to tell them to go get money because they knew they needed money to get the monkey (heroin) off their backs.

Ten years later and I'm now twenty-six and living large; so I thought.  I brought my mother a home and I'm living in my own house with all the amenities and a woman whom I thought was going to be my wife, although the relationship was a brought one.  However, at the time I didn't know that was what I was doing.  Money can't buy love and I found that out later in life because the woman I had fallen in love with was not in love with me, but the material gain.

I would buy her whatever she wanted.  For instance, a Mercedes Convertible, the best designer clothes, shoes, and she could travel and go where ever she wanted to go: Las Vegas, Cancun, Mexico, Paris, Italy, and even the Kentucky Derby where I first came to know about Louisville, Kentucky.  Kentucky was not only the home of the thoroughbred horses, but beautiful women which were my greatest weakness.

I thought that with my money I could have any female of consenting age that looked appealing to me. I thought I was rich, but I was only "nigga rich", which means to me ignorant; thinking all females are material item seekers and have to depend on the male to provide for them. I believed this up until the time I arrived in Louisville.

The city has quite a few independent women who make their own money – college graduates with good paying jobs. Thanks to good parenting, I guess, but it was different for me to have women not needing a man to provide room and board for them. All they needed was a male to give them good sex! This was my cup of tea at the time and without being a pimp, I guess it was more like being a gigolo.

Well, my woman of eight years, Sarah, grew up with me in the housing projects. Therefore, she was used to the male providing for her because she came from an environment that did not allow women to be independent. When I came to Louisville I was introduced to a new experience. I was surrounded by independent young, strong females who made their own money whether it was working at McDonald's or in Corporate America.

Those type of females let me know the real when it came to a female being with you because she wanted to be with you or so that you can take care of them. But fellas, you have to understand that if you're doing something illegal that there is a 50/50 chance that the female may go off to the next man to provide for her. And if she has kids, the odds are even greater because we, guys, have hurt them more than we've helped them by having them become dependent upon us.

So, when we get busted and go to jail; they move on. We can't be mad, get out and retaliate by killing the girl, the guy, or both because we created the monster so to speak. Therefore, we must move on with our lives and become a positive force in the society.

Moving to Louisville is what woke me up in regards to seeing that females could survive as independent women instead of dependents. Well, my meeting an independent woman caused my relationship with my dependent one to go sour.

Sarah started sending me to jail, taking money from me and hiding it. Sarah couldn't accept me wanting out of our relationship and if she couldn't have me then no one would. This caused me to become angry because I had given her too much information about myself and my business. Her attitude was that she had dirt on me and the only way I was leaving her was if I went to prison, got killed or just flat out died.

Sarah's dependency took me through a lot of unnecessary changes and basically because I allowed them to happen. Sarah's plotting and scheming messed up my program with a woman we'll call Madame X. Madame X was my independent woman who said she could not be with me until I was completely finished with Sarah. She explained to me that she wasn't interested in the extra drama.

It was really bothering me to the point that I wanted to talk to my mama about it, but I couldn't. Now, Sarah was pregnant and this was her way of keeping me or holding onto the relationship and not losing me to another woman. However, that was not in God's plan because she miscarried and I ended up having an affair with one of Sarah's girlfriends whom she had met during our stay in the 'Ville. Well, that friend became pregnant and gave birth to my daughter nine months later.

I didn't know anything about the baby until it was born and I was just as shocked as Sarah, but I must say that I took it a lot better than she did. That incident made her go over the edge, mildly speaking, and she was raving about how she couldn't believe that I had slept with her girlfriend and had a baby with her. She wanted revenge!

She raided my stash and took close to seventy thousand dollars from me. You have to admit…that was one sweet revenge. I confronted her about the money and of course she tried to pretend like she didn't have a clue as to its whereabouts. Well, then I clocked out! She went to the police again and I got locked up.

The prosecutor talked her into having me charged with stalking (she was fine as wine, but very conniving). I should have listened to the police officer from years before along with my friends when they told me that my best bet was to leave her alone. You know they say love is blind and I actually thought that I loved her. I know now that it wasn't love. It was more lust than anything. The sexual healing that she was giving me was better than I had received from any of the other females I had been with in the past.

This message goes out to the guys.

We can't let our little head out think our big head. It can get us into a lot of unwanted trouble. Also, females you can't let a guy control you with sex or else the same results may occur in your situation. Folks, all I'm saying is play as fair as possible and when you see that it is not a fair relationship anymore you must call it quits.

I became bitter with myself and then I concluded that regardless of what happened to have the female sex on this earth is a blessing. I accepted that what happened between Sarah and I was just as much her fault as mine. I concluded that men and women must communicate to make a relationship endure.

All I wanted was to make enough money so I could purchase my mom a home and in June of 2000 I did just that. I purchased the home, got her out of the projects, off the streets, and in (then out) of a drug treatment program. She has been clean for five years. My life, even though it was prosperous, was a total catastrophe due to Sarah's vindictiveness regarding the desire to dissolve our relationship. Unlike myself, she had become addicted to our lavish lifestyle and I just wanted to start over with someone who was capable of spoiling me as much as I was spoiling her.

Sarah wasn't going to make it that easy for me. She talked me into making an unusual cocaine purchase. She said after we sold the cocaine we would go our separate ways because with that much cash we would be set for the rest of our lives. I didn't know that it would be the last time I would see the streets for several years because I got busted and was charged with trafficking cocaine while Sarah got off. I knew she set me up and this was her saying that if she couldn't have me no one would.

Now, I'm here serving a twenty year sentence with an eligibility for parole in about thirteen.

Young people, all I'm saying is the time is not worth the crime. Breaking the law is not worth spending your life in some prison institution. Now, all I can do is pray and hope that one day I will be released from behind these walls to start a family, get a job, and see my kids grow up. Until then, I just say one day a change is going to come.

You all have a chance to direct your own lives. Which direction will you choose? Believe me this is not the direction to take. I would rather be a poor man not having to look over his shoulder than a rich man wondering what the next day will bring due to his dealings in drugs or any criminal activity.

Plus, if you know what I know you will pursue your dreams in a positive manner. Sure, I said that I dreamed of moving my mother from the projects into a nice home, but I didn't expand my dreams to other means. I could have been an engineer, singer, doctor, or an athlete. I succeeded in getting my mom a house, but I failed at setting my sights on positive goals for myself.

Now, I've gotten my G.E.D. along with a masonry trade. I'm on the list for small engine repair and I would like to make a positive move with my life. One of the main things I learned from being incarcerated is that you can use your time wisely, such as, thinking about what your purpose is in life and what you would do if you were given the opportunity for freedom.

My thoughts seem to always go back to what I could have done to prevent me from coming this route in the first place. Of course, that was something I didn't think about when I was free; the consequences of my actions. So, if you think about committing a crime, you must also realize the consequence that may occur from the crime in which you commit. I would like to stress to you that it is not worth giving up your freedom for quick cash because you are not guaranteed to walk out from behind these prison walls.

Behind these prison walls lay some of the most notorious criminals in the world that are never going to get out of society again and will kill you as soon as you disrespect them or their space. You never know what may tick them off and your life is at stake because these folks do not care and this goes for male or female convicts. I mean some convicts do not repent, they just get angrier and you could become their next victim. They feel they have nothing to lose anyway because they are already in for life.

It's a marriage to the institution until death causes them to part. Don't come this way unless you are a hard headed individual who wants nothing more out of life than to become institutionalized. My advice is to pursue another path or travel another road because life is short enough and to give it to the system would be completely foolish.

Youngsters, if you have a friend and you see him or her drifting into a negative situation…talk to them! Ask them questions until you get some response as to why they are choosing that particular route. Call their parents, teacher, counselor, preacher or even the police, especially if it will prevent them from committing a crime that could cost them their life. I'm not saying be a snitch; I am saying save your friend's life! That is, if you care about them.

Personally, I wouldn't have been here if I had listened to my mother's plea with me about the direction I was going with my life. So, if you hear…please, take heed to my plea to you. Now, ask yourselves a question – would you rather leave school to go to prison and have guards telling you where you can and cannot go and what you can and cannot do? Or would you rather make those choices on your own?

School is an outing in the park compared to prison.

You all can make a difference in our society and slow the prison population down by making the right decisions in your lives because once you cross the line there is no guarantee that you will return. Remember, the choice is yours and you are the director of your own path. Don't get suckered into peer pressure and remember that everything that glitters is not necessarily gold. I'm living proof of that.

I'm sure you've heard the saying, "Go with your first instinct." Our instincts are never wrong. When something doesn't feel right, don't do it! My being here in the system has really made me realize that doing illegal things is not worth being here. If I live to see my release day, I will try to help boys and girls overcome negative objectives so they will know that there are other alternatives. I have seen men die in here!

I have seen guys incarcerated, released and back in a year because of new charges or parole violations, which is one of the reasons why the jails are overcrowded; because of the parole officers hired by the government who are not looking out for the parolee's best interest and the parolee testing the system.

The system did pass a new law that allows inmates to "walk off" their time on the streets. This means that if they get revoked for a parole violation, the time spent on the streets (free) still counts towards the original time left on the shelf.

Again, my advice is to not do the crime because it is not worth the time. Believe me, I know! We must have confidence in ourselves and society to achieve the goals we set in our lives, which come with commitment, so stay focused to whatever is positive in your life.

When I was coming up I stayed focused, but I was focused on the negative. Pimping and drug dealing which had proven to be the wrong road for me. It cost me my freedom and that is time that I can never replace. Therefore, you all can make the right decision to be positive or negative, right or wrong. It's not about doing, in my opinion, really it's about being able to live a life that will allow you to grow without worrying about the law coming to take your possessions along with your freedom; or someone who is jealous of your prosperity and comes to rob you or your family of drugs plus your money.

I'm not saying you couldn't possibly get robbed living a honest clean life, but if you do you can contact the proper authorities and have them investigate so they may recover your property in contrast to not being able to tell them you got robbed for drugs and money, and then you're looking at jail plus possible prison time.

All I'm saying again is that crime doesn't pay enough for you all, from my experience to do time. It's just not worth it once you get put on the other side of the fence and cannot leave when you want, you're no longer in charge of your life, the prison system is the head of your household, and to sum it all up...do not be foolish and stubborn like I was.  Make the right choices and learn to hear from listening.

The Runner


Chapter IV – Prison Talk From Leon


Hello, my name is Leon and I'm from Lexington, Kentucky. I'm here at Northpoint Training Center doing ten years for distribution of crack cocaine. It is now March, 2003 and I've been here since July, 2000, with no parole hearing as of yet. I would like to share some of my life's experiences with you all in hopes that maybe it will steer you down another road. I was born in December, 1982 and was raised in a single-parent household with my mother in Douglas Projects.

I grew up seeing my mother struggle, to be honest, and she was poor, uneducated, and from a broken home. My mother's parents worked hard to support her and her two brothers, but due to my granddaddy having other women, my granny divorced him because the money he was spending on those other women was taking away from her kids. Sadly enough, my granddaddy was said to have fathered other children, but enough about them…

My story goes like this.

Since I was old enough to remember (which was about eight years old), I saw my mother go through boyfriend after boyfriend. As I previously stated she was uneducated, but my mom's was very pretty and drew the attention of the guys who were known to have a little money. However, all she would get out of them was a roll in the sack and a small piece of crack to smoke. Her actions hurt me because our refrigerator stayed empty. It stayed empty until the first of the month came along and she would buy some groceries with her food stamps, and then the rest of them, along with her welfare check, would go towards the purchase of crack cocaine.

My mom was like sixteen when she had me, so we kinda grew up together. When I was eight she was twenty-four and she was as fine as any of the females in these videos. My father is unknown. I have no clue who he is. I've seen some pictures of him from my mother's concert days (before she became a crack head), when she would go out and shine, you know? Party.

As she grew older and pressed, from having me and my father leaving her, it seemed like all she would do was see how many crack dealers she could sleep with. This seemed like power because those were the only guys she'd have sex with. As I keep talking about my mom; she is still fine. I guess that came from good genes. Ha.

Plus, these dudes had sharp rides, nice clothes, and what seemed like plenty of money. Some of the dudes would give me a bet (a couple of dollars) to get some candy and a pop. There was one brother who stood out because it seemed like he was really feeling my mom's. He would always ask her to slow down on the crack, give her money to get groceries, and take us shopping for clothes. I will not reveal his name, but we'll call him Mr. Pablo and he was a true gentleman towards my mom and me.

# The Runner

I chose the drug/cocaine dealing as my lifestyle but did not realize it was going to land me in prison; later to serve ten years of my life to the department of corrections. This place has to be the lowest part of my life because I had a choice to do right, but I chose to do wrong and must serve my time. Simply because you may come from a household of low income, believe me, selling dope has a much higher price to pay than being poverty stricken. You may see profit in the beginning, but in the end, you will still be a loser. You'll either lose your life to the streets or your freedom to the penal system.

If I had a chance to press rewind, I would not have dealt with cocaine or anything else illegal for that matter, especially, if I knew it would cost me my freedom.

My routine was that I would go to school to learn my lessons, cut grass in the spring and summer months, rake leaves in the fall, and then shovel snow in the winter; at least until I turned fourteen. It was then I would get a job while attending school, learn how to play sports and be all that I could be.

Unfortunately, we can't press rewind. What's done is done. Our lives are not equipped with buttons to control our fate and this is why I'm sharing this valuable information with you and would like to thank Mr. Runner for giving me the opportunity to do so.

Well, it was 1994 and I was twelve years old when I sold my first piece of cocaine. I stole it out of my mom's pack so I could get something to eat and it happened to sell for $20. From that day forward, my career in the dope game began.

The drug transaction made me feel so powerful and you must understand that I knew exactly where to go and get the sale because we had what they called the dope stroll and just about everyone knew who I was. There was no problem for me as far as blending in was concerned, but they did not know I came down on the stroll that day as a seller. That was cool with me because I didn't want them to know and tell my mother I was on the dope stroll selling crack cocaine. The way I got on was with the ten dollars I had left from the twenty after I purchased some food.

I brought what you call a double-up from one of my young buddies, who was just a couple years older than I, but he had been selling for a while and knew my living situation and helped me come up or at least I thought at the time. We kept it on the down low from my mom's for quite some time. Then one day I was slipping, so to speak, and she happened to be washing my clothes early one Saturday morning.

She checked my pants pockets and found $250 plus, three grams of crack cocaine. I recall those were the pants I had on Friday night. I had put a lot of money in them and forgot to put it up. Well, my mother taught me a lesson. She pretended not to know anything and kept the money, plus smoked the crack cocaine. Therefore, it caused me to confront her about what she did and her response to me was, "How dare you try and sell crack and not tell me?  That's what you get and be careful out on the stroll for the police and robbers because it's against the law and it's a dirty game, son."

In other words, she gave me the green light to get money, which at the time I thought was cool, but I now know it was not. My mother should have whipped my ass, excuse my language, but that's what should have been done.  Plus, she should have turned me over to the children's justice system to deter me from selling crack cocaine.  They could have dealt with me then instead of now, but I can't press rewind, so this is why I'm glad I can share my learning experience with you all.

Hopefully, I can make a difference in some person's life, so that they will know the drugs or crime doesn't pay enough for doing time or losing your life.  When I was only twelve, I thought I was being a man about it.  I was only setting myself up for self-destruction.  I stopped doing well in my school work.  I would just do enough to get by because it was too much due to my new job and the hours I was working (oh yes, it's a job and a dangerous one too).  I was so good at selling crack cocaine and eventually that was all I wanted to do.

This went on for about three years without any incidents occurring that involved me.  That was until one day I was on my job during the summer months, serving crack and a car came through looking to score some dope.  I was excited, but I was also young and aggressive which didn't make to be a very good combination in this game. One time this driver pulled up on the stroll and asked me to get in the car because he had a lot of money to spend, but didn't want to get robbed. When he flashed a wad of cash in my face I got in the car.

Being greedy almost cost me my life because he locked the doors and pulled off. Then he pulled out a forty-five caliber hand gun and told me to take off my pants, socks, and shoes or else he was going to blow my head off. I did as he said and then he told me to open the door and get out! I told myself from that day on no one would catch me without a gun again. After that incident I went and purchased my first handgun; a forty-five caliber like the one the driver had. This started my collection of firearms.

I knew that if I was going to be in the game, I had to have protection because the game isn't always what it seems to be. I mean, it looks good with all the money, jewelry, clothes and rides, but your life is at a greater risk than if you were just walking down the street coming from a regular nine to five or school. In the dope game, you don't just have the police; you have the DEA coming for you, the gangsta wanna be's, the dope fiends, and other drug dealers wanting to take you out.

Youngsters, don't be stupid and try to play this game because you cannot win in the end. I got myself caught up deeper in the game when I purchased that gun.

I flashed it and word got around that I was packing and since I was a minor, I figured that I would get away with juvenile time if I had to use it on somebody. This gave me a reputation as being hard, but in reality I was scared and trying to protect what was mine.

1998 and I'm sixteen years of age and moving up in the cocaine distribution game. It was now time to really floss. I had to get my driving permit, and then my license so I could purchase a hot automobile…and I mean hot! The car had me hotter than July because at the time I thought what I was doing was cool, but it just made me a much bigger target. I purchased a new BMW 325I.

The car itself made me more aggressive towards selling coke. Another mistake I made was that I quit school. I was staying up later due to my transportation and the fiends that would call or come by during the wee hours of the morning. When they stopped coming and calling it was usually around eight or nine in the morning. I would get some breakfast and sleep until six or seven that evening and be at it again. Sunday was my only off day.

My motto was, "Money over school, broads and my freedom!" That was the other mistake I made. You know, I actually thought what I was doing was okay and it definitely was not cool at all. It was a total catastrophe. I became obsessed with making money and that's all I thought life was about and it's not what life is about at all to me now. Unfortunately, I had to learn from inside these prison walls that life has more to offer than just making money from selling drugs for material gain. My life revolved around how much money I could make in one day, week and month.

# Learn To Hear From Listening

Now that I'm here in prison I know that there are other avenues to pursue regarding making money legally e.g. brick layer, electrician, and small engine repair man. If not one of these then I can pursue several other trades. I can even continue my education. One thing I know for sure is that I will not be involved with selling drugs or doing anything illegal again. Time spent behind bars is not worth my freedom and besides they are giving away football jersey numbers for drug distributions, which means a lot of time.

Doing my fling with selling cocaine I remember thinking, "I just want to make money and buy all the things my mother and father didn't get for me or couldn't afford." Like I said, my mother used crack and was uneducated. She was all I had at home and I loved her and still do, but I made sure she did not want for nothing. She could have abandoned me at any time when I was born but she didn't and I will be forever in her debt. Without her, there would be no me. I'm not proud of the lifestyle she lived, but I'm proud to be her son and learn at an early age that life is too short to continue to stay stuck on stupid. I was stupid at the time of my drug selling.

To think that I could go and buy whatever my cash money allowed me to buy and think that I wouldn't be noticed by friends, enemies, and the law enforcement agencies was naïve. That caused me to become hot and that became my blessing in disguise. Had it not been for me drawing attention to myself I may have still been out there in the streets - still selling or dead.

The Runner

I now have my G.E.D. and I'm in brick masonry school. So, you can make a wrong turn or a right turn. The way you all go is up to you.

As for me, I'm hoping I get to walk out of these gates a free man, but until then I continue to stay strong and focused on the prize, which is freedom. Hopefully, the future will bring that for me, however from 1998 until January, 2000, I kept having run-ins with the law. I should have learned to hear from listening to an old wine head from my neighborhood. He told me that I was better than selling drugs and to stay in school and get an education. It seemed my run-ins with the law kept adding up after my first arrest.

My first arrest, I was charged with possession of one piece of crack cocaine and I went to the juvenile detention center. My mom had to come and get me out. Then, I had a court date where I told them that I found the crack. They gave me a slap on the wrist and after that, I thought I was untouchable. This led to more arrests for possession of crack all totaling about seven times from the time I was sixteen until I turned twenty years of age.

The judge finally got tired of seeing me come in and leave with a simple slap on the wrist and since I was no longer a juvenile I had to pay to play. In other words, I had to pay for a good lawyer and he had to share money or favors with the prosecutor and judge over my cases. All of this could have been avoided if only I had listened. Instead, I let it go in one ear and out the other. I mean it's a no win situation.

You may get away for a while and pay a lawyer a lot of money to keep you out of jail or prison, but sooner or later his favors will run out and you will find out that all prosecutors and judges are not crooked. They just uphold the law by the oath that they took. So, you can't be mad at no one but yourself for doing the crime. Hopefully, you all will get this message and make the right decision with your lives. Believe me, I must confess and am a living witness that crime is not worth doing time! People, young and old, I hope you all get this message because it's not about being tough or scared it's about learning to hear from listening to what is positive and right. Thank you all for reading my short story!

## Chapter V – Prison Talk From Kenneth

Hello, my name is Kenneth and I'm speaking to you all about myself on May 4, 2003 here at Northpoint Training Center. I'm a white male who has been in the system since I was eleven years old. This is my fourth trip to serve in prison and I will die here this time; unless some miracle happens.

I'm forty years of age and I became institutionalized the first time I got locked up. What makes it so weird is that I didn't even know it because I was only eleven. I was doing what I thought would get me accepted by my peers, who in my neighborhood, were all a couple of years older than myself.

I grew up in a small country town in Kentucky. I will not give the name of the town to keep from further embarrassing my mother and father, who gave me a good life; a life full of opportunity to advance. However, I was an only child and, to me, at the time I was growing up I felt they sheltered me and pampered me so, when I did get out, I was buck wild. I remember my first arrest. The guys dared me to steal five pair of socks from the Dollar Store in the middle of the summer.

Well, I got caught and being from a small town, we did not have a children detention center so, they took me to jail with the grown men. They called my parents to inform them of what had happened and when my parents found out they were outraged! My mom was crying and my dad asked me what got into me? He asked me were they not doing enough for me; didn't I have plenty of socks at home? I shook my head, yes.

At the time of my arrest, I remember being scared when they told me they were taking me to jail with grown men and I started crying. When I got to the station and found out they couldn't put me in the cells with the men because I was a minor and I was pleased. My dad put me under punishment for a whole month and that merely consisted of not going outside to play. By it being a small town, just about everyone knew I had gotten arrested. The lock up situation got me to become a made guy, because I didn't snitch (rat, tell) on the other guys who had put me up to the dare.

After I came off my punishment, I was told this by the guys and at that time my life, it made me feel real good about myself. It made me feel good that I had gone to jail and became a gang member because I didn't tell no one. However, this only made matters worse. Since I was a minor, the only thing that would happen to me was go to jail and wait on my parents to come and get me. I continued that path for two years.

I was stealing and getting caught, however, I didn't get caught all the time, but I got caught one time too many. My parents couldn't control my destiny and I was sent to juvenile camp for bad boys where I resided until the age of sixteen. While I was locked down, I met some seemingly cool guys, but they just led me into more trouble. I'm not blaming anyone for my mistakes, but back then, I was easily misled because I wanted so desperately to fit in.

At sixteen I quit school and started stealing cars because the money was pretty good to me at the time. Shoot, three or four thousand for thirty minutes tops…I was good at boosting cars and the payout was incredible! I became known as a car thief and my very own mouth got me caught. I would brag about how good I was, not knowing at the time that I should have kept my mouth shut about my business. If I had been listening to my parents, I wouldn't have been in that line of work at all!

The police got tipped off about me making a pick-up of some vehicles and followed me until I made my auto heist. Then they busted me dead in the act! I got five years for that; two in juvenile, until I was eighteen, but if I stayed clean while there they would put me on probation for the other three. Well, I stayed straight while in juvenile, but as soon as they released me I was back at it again.

It seemed like I got a rush out of doing crime, plus I had added muscle to my slim frame. I weighted almost two hundred pounds and stood six foot three inches tall. I started making guys work for me just as I had gotten accustomed to in juvenile detention - the smaller guys paid me for protection. When I got on the streets I used the very same method to get extra money. At the time I thought it was a cool thing to do, but in reality it was wrong and I wouldn't do that to no one again.

Youngsters, you all can make the right choices. You don't have to follow the paths that many of us have and become institutionalized. The crime does not compare to the time that you will receive once you're caught. Listen to me! My parents provided for me and I came from a good family. However, I still wanted to be accepted by my supposed to be friends. They turned out not to be friends at all because they were, and then they would have been giving me positive and not negative advice.

My freedom no longer exists in this lifetime. Do you want to be in this situation? Believe me...I don't! But I put myself here by not listening to my parents and teachers. I find myself in a trance sometimes, thinking that one day I'll be out of here. Reality is that I don't know if I'm ever leaving...not alive. Then I think back to the act that got me stuck here. These are some of the other events that brought me here for life.

I started doing burglaries in other cities. I would case out fruit stands and junk yards because these folks were getting some tax free money. They were put in a tax bracket so there is no way the IRS could keep up with the sales they generated. For instance, if they sold one hubcap at the same price as they would sell four, but still had the remaining three, they could sell the other three at the same price or for more or less. In any event, there is no recording of these types of sales.

Those folks would usually keep the money in their homes in a wall safe, stuffed inside a bed mattress, vacuum cleaner bag or somewhere in their homes and to me it was an easy hustle. I got away with it a few times ant eh money was good. However, one day I got caught thanks to what they call ADT, the silent alarm system. That sent me back five years because I didn't have a firearm on me and no one was home, therefore no one's life was in danger. So, the system tapped me on the wrist with five years.

I went and did my time, learned more about how to be a criminal and served out. I did good for awhile, but the money was coming too slow for me on a regular nine to five job and I turned back to a life of crime. I committed home burglaries, again, using the same methods as before, but this time I knew how to deactivate the alarm system. Well, this time I got out and stayed straight for about two years and then, I was back at it again. This time I thought I would step my game up, but instead I stepped right back into the system. I was attempting to rob a grocery store and shot and killed the clerk. This is why I am now serving life in prison without the possibility of parole. The plea I accepted stopped me from getting the death penalty.

So, I would advise you folks who are free to think about the consequences that come with committing a crime. Don't do the crime if you do not want to lose your freedom for life or even one day. It's not worth it! There are too many opportunities in life to waste it on a life of crime. I'm a living witness, but you have to make the choice to do right or do wrong. I made this choice when I disregarded my parents. They tried their best to direct me in the right direction in life. They gave me the finer things until I decided to go beyond their reach; outside of their love, a place to live and, to the best of their ability, security.

Here I am at Northpoint Training Center, stuck until the day I die, and watching guys come and go as I did. If they keep coming and going they too will have the door slammed shut behind them without it ever opening again. That's how the law works…it's their job. Same as someone who has to go to a nine to five; they have to uphold the law to the best of their ability.

I'm not saying the system is flawless because it's not. Until or if it ever becomes flawless, we have to play by their rules and this goes back to learning to hear from listening to your parents, teachers, coaches, and even our own conscious. We know when we are doing something that we are not supposed to be doing. I, being my own worst enemy, have no one to blame, but myself. I was not thinking about the real consequences that would come my way if I kept doing illegal activities. I really thought this was a joke because I'd come and gone so much that my mind became institutionalized.

I thought I knew what to expect from the prison system and it was routine for me to do a little time, meet more convicts, learn more criminal acts, and then get released and go home. Well, that last criminal act cost me my freedom for the rest of my life. There is no getting out this time! I will do time until I die.

I can't say this enough to all who are free from bondage. Stay that way! Believe me, I would trade places with a soldier fighting war for another chance at freedom.

People we need to address ourselves when we feel like doing some criminal activity. We need to ask ourselves is it worth it. Especially, when there is a chance that you could be killed or caught and have to do time. I'd rather flip hamburgers at McDonald's than do a crime and be locked down for the rest of my life as I am now. For me that chance is over and the thought is merely a dream, but for you it's not.

Pay attention and do the right thing and your chances of coming this route are slim to none. Make the most of life by staying in school instead of dropping out; thinking it's cool and you're grown. You're cool, in my opinion, when you achieve your goals in life and become anything in the world that you want to be e.g. a doctor, lawyer, nurse, professional athlete, etc. Make sure it's legal and you enjoy doing what you do because being a prison inmate is not the career to choose.

Do not be like me and rebel against the ones who love and want nothing but success for you. We need to help one another when we're able to; no matter your skin color or gender.

I spent a lot of my life trying to commit hideous crimes and this is where it landed me. I spent time sharing knowledge with guys coming in here for the first time, and to guys who also have another chance at freedom; trying to explain to them that this is not the way to spend their lives. I let them know that they have more to offer to society than just getting three hot meals and a cot from the state correctional department.

I let them know they can make a difference in society, if they put themselves to use in a positive manner; take up a trade, go back to school and get their G.E.D., enroll into college or even get a job washing dishes or flipping burgers…anything that's legal and will keep them from coming into the judicial system. I explain to them they can cut grass in the spring and summer, rake leaves in the fall and although it may not be a lot of money…fast money (the things that most of us are accustomed to), but it will keep them from coming back here with no way out.

So, I'm asking you, if one of your friends seem to be heading in the wrong direction, DO NOT be afraid to tell them that they are headed down the wrong path. A true friend will speak up and say what's on their minds no matter what the consequences may be. Or if you have a sibling heading in the wrong direction, let them know before it's too late. Even an adult may need some guidance, if so, speak to them in a respectful manner jut to let them know you care.

Hopefully, I've made a difference in your outlook on life by sharing this with you. Thank you very much for listening.

Sincerely, Darryl.

## Chapter VI – Prison Talk From Mark

Hello, my name is Mark and I'm serving time here at Northpoint Training Center for rape and sodomy. I have about fifteen years left to serve. I'm also from a city here in Kentucky and I was raped and sodomized from the time I was old enough to remember, which was about eight. I grew up thinking this was normal because my father was doing this to me and he's a Catholic priest. I grew up not knowing this was a cruel and unusual act, not to mention punishment, and this went on for ten years.

When I was entering my ninth grade year in high school, I experienced or committed my first sexual assault on a smaller male, who was on the track team with me. The two of us were the last ones in the shower and I approached him and began to kiss him in the mouth. I was much bigger and stronger than him, so I overpowered him by putting my arms around his neck and choking him until he became unconscious. Then I took my middle finger and stuck it up his anus. For some reason I got an erection and then that was when I inserted my penis causing feces and blood to discharge out. After that I took off running.

I went home and told my father what I had done and he told me not to worry that he would take care of me. He told me not to tell what he had done to me because if I did they would take me away from him.

Later on that evening the police came to our house and locked me up. Since I was a juvenile, my dad could come down and sign for my release; contingent upon him brining me to appear in court whenever my court date was set. When I went back to court the judge told me that they were going to send me away to a mental hospital for treatment because I was sick. If I completed the program, I would not have to do time when I reached the rightful age of eighteen. I completed the evaluation and sex offender program. That only made me more sick because me and another minor were the only kids in the program and the rest were adults and they were all professionals: priests, doctors, teachers, and a few lawyers.

These were people who we trust a great deal not only with grown-ups but with kids as well. That seemed to confirm what my father would say to me, "it's alright son." Well, come to find out those folks were molested as children as well and never told anyone until they became adults or attacked other innocent kids and got caught.

When I got out, my dad convinced me to let him have his way with me again. When he finished with me I would go clean myself up and go out to daycare centers in search for potential sex partners, who were outside playing and could be easily tempted by candy for favors.

I started saving my money so that I could move away from home to another city or state as long as I could be out of my parents' house. Finally, I had saved enough money from working and turning tricks to move out and into my own apartment. While I was in treatment I got my high school diploma and now, since I had my own apartment and tricks, I enrolled into college.

When I started college, my attitude towards tricks diminished. I started talking to females who were loners and I would sneak up behind the girl at night when she would be in an isolated area, approach her from behind, and then inject her with a tranquilizer. I would then carry her to my car and have my way with her. Afterwards, I would dump the body away from campus at a park.

Sometimes, I would approach small males, who were loners, and give them the same treatment; depending on my frame of mind that night. I attacked my victims at night because that was the best opportunity for me not to be seen by any witnesses. I got away with my sick adventures for about two semesters, and then I got caught thanks to good ole' campus security and the police sending out decoys.

This time I was over eighteen and away from home with a history of being a sex offender. The judge made an example of me because of the severity of the crime. I realize now that I was the victim who victimized innocent people and I have the opportunity to let the readers of this book know that if you are victims – tell the proper authorities so that you will no longer be hurt or hurt other innocent people.

Me, I'm a sick individual because of someone who helped give me life and whom the public looked to for assistance. I will not be able to live a normal life in this world due to the damage that was done to me. No matter how hard I try, I always seem to have nightmares about the way I was raised. However, like I said, you can stop the madness before it's too late.

I do not know what I'll do if they release me, however, the judge ordered me to receive treatment. I'm a sex offender who was taught that is was okay to take sex from males and females. Sometimes, I think that I'll make it out of here safe because if these guys in here find out I'm a pedophile they'll kill me! They don't like child molesters or rapists in here.

Thank you readers for letting me say a little something. Hopefully, I can help save other people from being hurt. Learn to hear from listening. Even if it's your conscious talking!

## Chapter VII – Prison Talk Final Destination

People of the world today, you all have choices as to your life's final destination. What choices will you make? Prison, be killed or live life until to its fullest? It's that simple. Yes, accidents do happen, but the percentage is not a high enough rate for you to blame every single misfortune on an *accident*. So, think before you act and thank you all for reading this book. I hope you will learn to hear from listening…and reading!

# Learn To Hear From Listening

The Runner

About the Author

The Runner was born and raised in Louisville, KY where he currently resides.

To correspond with The Runner or to book him to speak at your event:

Email: TheRunner502@gmail.com